THE TR ACCO␣␣␣␣␣T

HOW TO HAVE ␣␣␣␣␣SSFUL
ACCOUNTINɢ ␣AREER

STER_ING
CHARTERED
ACCOUNTANT L_BS

Level 33, 25 Canada Square,

Canary Wharf, London E14 5LQ

handbooks@sterlinglibs.com

www.sterlinglibs.com

All rights reserved. No part of this book may be reproduced or transmitted in any form or by any means, electronic or mechanical, including photocopying, recording or by any information storage and retrieval system, without written permission from the author, except for inclusion of brief quotations for review.

Unattributed quotations are by Sterling Libs

Copyright © 2015 by Sterling Libs

Editions ISBNs

Softcover		CD/Video		Audio,MP3
978-0-9931977-3-4	■	*978-0-9931977-8-9*	■	*978-0-9931977-9-6*

I

Table of Contents

About the Author

Sterling Libs FCCA, is a fellow of the Association of Chartered Certified Accountants and the author of more than 5 books on practical accountancy and on how to succeed as an accounting professional.

He runs his own accounting firm in Canary Wharf London.

Sterling is so passionate about helping young aspiring accounting professionals to better understand how accounting is done in practice.

He has championed UK practical work experience in accountancy training which has helped many individuals - (ACCA students & Affiliates, AAT students, CIMA students/Affiliates, university students and graduates in accounting and also those who are already working but want more in-depth practical experience in accounting), and as a direct result many of them have got accounting jobs in the UK.

Sterling is really gifted in making the seemingly complex simple and throughout his books he shows you fundamental and detailed illustrations with examples of how he does that.

He is an inspiring individual.

Preface – Note to the reader

Accounting is a very dynamic profession and if you desire a future of constant growth and change then accounting will certainly provide that for you. Not to mention the financial rewards, the personal and professional rewards are quite impressive too.

An accountant can fill many different business positions and roles. The opportunities are great and you can actually find that perfect job – the job just for you. You can work for yourself, work in an accounting firm, in a company in a particular industry, or government, to name but a few.

Accountants are needed in all areas of the economy. You are likely to be seen as a valuable core member of the finance team in many of the organisations with their own finance department.

The chances of you finding work are significantly high as successful companies will always need accounting staff to work in their finance departments.

Different sectors and employers all have their own advantages and disadvantages – you have to decide what suits your personality and career aspirations best.

I believe this book will be a very invaluable resource to you as you get a head start on your accounting career.

Sterling Geoff Libs FCCA, ACPA, MAAT

Warning & disclaimer

This book is designed to provide information on how you can start well in your practical accounting career. It is sold with the understanding that the publisher and author are not engaged in rendering legal, accounting or other professional services. If legal or other expert assistance is required, the services of a competent professional should be sought.

It is not the purpose of this book to reprint all information that is otherwise available to accounting students, trainees, graduates or any other accounting professionals, but instead to complement, amplify and supplement other texts. You are urged to read all available material that you can find on this subject and tailor the information to your individual needs.

Every effort has been made to make the information in this book as complete and accurate as possible. However, there may be mistakes, both typographical and in content. Therefore, this text should be used only as a general guide and not as the ultimate source of getting started well in your accounting career. Furthermore, this book contains information on accounting specific for trainee accountants that is current only up to the printing date.

The purpose of this book is to educate and entertain. The author and publisher shall have neither liability nor responsibility to any person or entity with respect to loss or damage caused, or alleged to have been caused, directly or indirectly, by the information contained in this book

If you do not wish to be bound by the above, you may return this book to the publisher for a full refund before continuing to read any further or making use of the information in this book.

INTRODUCTION

There aren't many careers as diverse as accountancy. Not only can you train in business, practice or banking, but once qualified accountants are found working in high level jobs all over the world.

Working in accounting whether as a bookkeeper, accounts assistant, management accountant, or financial accountant requires training at academic, professional and practical levels.

You will be embarking on your career to gain work experience at many of the organisations out there having successfully completed the academic stage or just about being done. The work experience in the "real world" outside the college or university is designed to give you an understanding of the nature and role of the accounting profession and to develop a strong sense of professionalism.

A major function of the work experience training you will go through is to draw out and develop your academic intellectual and personal skills and resources, shaping and adapting them to the resolution of practical accounting problems.

Whether you have come directly from the comparatively unstructured life of a student at university or have been holding responsible positions or have not taken part in formal training for many years, I hope to smooth out your understanding of the fundamental principles of practical accounting and in that respect I will start from the basics or from the "ground up" so as to help you adjust to understanding how accounting works in practice.

Why choose accounting as a career

High salaries

Many accountancy trainees can double their salary during their training agreement. Salaries for newly qualified professional accountants for example compare favourably with salaries for careers in law, general management and banking.

Opportunity

Being an accountant will give you the competitive edge in employment. 81% of FTSE 100 companies have at least one Chartered Accountant on their board.

Security

The accountancy industry is buoyant even in a difficult economic climate, and accountants enjoy a more stable career than other finance professionals.

Flexibility

Being an accountant opens many doors. After qualifying you could go on to work in the highest levels of accounting, finance or business.

A global career

You'll have opportunities to work overseas especially as many of the professional qualifications like those provided by ICAEW, ACCA, and CIMA etc. are recognised around the world.

What I intend to do in this book is to give you the hands on fundamentals that you need to kick-start your career as an accountant in practice and industry.

You see, whatever you study theoretically in the colleges and universities should find its application in the businesses that are constantly building the economy.

You will also realise that not everything you study in the classroom will be applied at the same role in accounting unless of course you are the sole accountant in an organisation and are not working as part of a team in a finance department.

So, we are going to begin from scratch, I am going to assume you have never worked in practice at all and I will walk you through the key things you need to know as a fresher, if I may use that phrase, then build your practical understanding one step at a time.

Shall we begin?

ACCOUNTING JOBS & HOW TO GET THEM

Top 10 accounting jobs for you

Accountants are needed in all areas of the economy. You are likely to be seen as a valuable core member of the finance team in many organisations with a finance department.

The chances of you finding work are significantly high as successful companies will always need accounting staff to work in their finance departments.

Different sectors and employers all have their own advantages and disadvantages – you have to decide what suits your personality and career aspirations best.

Here are the top 10 jobs in accounting that you could potentially choose as a career path

i. Bookkeeper

Job profile: Most of the time you'll work 9am to 5pm, Monday to Friday. There may be the odd times when it's really quite busy (like during yearend) and you need to work a few extra hours.

Your main role is to maintain financial records for the company and to do your job effectively, you ought to have a detail-oriented approach to work that will allow you to keep up with company expenditures, income, and payroll as well as tax requirements.

There are positions across a wide range of organisations, so it's up to you to choose an industry you are interested in - health, public sector, private sector, charities etc.

There are opportunities for part-time and job sharing. Temporary work is often available too. You could also work freelance to work the hours that suit you.

The larger the company you work for, the more opportunities for progression there will be.

With experience and sufficient professional qualifications you could choose to be self-employed or set up your own company supporting several smaller businesses.

Salary: For a new starter you can expect to earn between £12,000 and £14,000 a year. As you get more experience you'll be able to earn up to £20,000. On average, for an experienced and qualified bookkeeper salary can be £23,000-£27,500 (Association for Accounting Technicians)

ii. Sales Ledger clerk

Job profile: Sales ledger clerks form the administrative side of an accounting team. You'll spend most of your time at your desk raising invoices and talking to clients.

This job is ideal for you if you want a career that offers room to move as there's plenty of scope for promotion once you've got some experience. Sales ledger clerks often graduate to work as a supervisor or manager and from there to credit controller and even financial controller.

Your main duties will include:

- *Setting up new clients*
- *Producing invoices*
- *Sorting out any rebates, posts and filing*
- *Running off turnover statements*
- *Banking and reconciliation*
- *Checking sales VAT has been included on invoices*
- *Chasing up outstanding debts*

Salary: Starting salary can be around £18,000 to £20,000. This will increase to £30,000 plus once you take on a more supervisory role.

iii. Purchase ledger clerk

Job profile: Typical work hours are 9:00am – 5:00pm Monday to Friday. Your responsibilities will depend on the size of the company you work for, and you may have sole control over payments or work as part of a much bigger purchase ledger team. Purchase ledger clerks are expected to be able to:

- *Code and check supplier invoices*
- *Work out VAT payments*

- *Check and reconcile supplier statements*
- *Pay out money via BACS or by cheque*
- *Deal with purchase enquiries*
- *File invoices and statements*
- *Process staff expenses*
- *Manage petty cash*

Salary: As a starter, you should expect your salary to range from £16,00-£23,000 per year, depending on your experience and qualifications.

iv. Accounts Assistant

Job profile: As an Accounts assistant you will provide administrative support to accountants, handling mail and basic bookkeeping and undertaking clerical tasks such as making phone calls, typing, and filing

Depending on the size of the organisation you work for, the tasks you will be performing include but not limited to:

- *Assisting with all aspects of sales & purchase ledger*
- *Assisting with the preparation of statutory accounts.*
- *Assisting with credit control and debtor management.*
- *Calculating and checking to make sure payments, amounts and records are correct.*
- *Working with spreadsheets and journals.*
- *Sorting out incoming and outgoing daily post and answering any queries.*

- *Managing petty cash transactions.*

- *Reconciling finance accounts and direct debits.*

- *Assisting with payroll and posting payroll journals*

Salary: Accounts assistants earn an average of £18,500 – £22,000 a year (for full-time hours), but the starting salary can be as little as £13, 000 for inexperienced employees.

v. Credit Controller

Job profile: This is primarily an office-based role where you'll be expected to work 9:00am -5:00pm, Monday to Friday with some overtime at busy periods such as the end of the year. The beauty of this role is that credit control principles are the same whatever industry you work in and you can move into different sectors. With enough experience you could even become the go to person – consultant.

It will be your responsibility to review debt recovery procedures and stop the supply of goods and services - or even start the serious process of legal action - if a client has paid late or missed multiple payments. It's not the nicest part of the job, but someone's got to do it. You may be required to attend meetings with clients or occasionally court hearings if you're taking legal action against a client.

Generally, your role will include performing the following tasks:

- *Ensuring customers pay on time*

- *Setting up the terms and conditions of credit to customers*

- *Deciding whether or not to offer the credit and how much to offer to a client*

- *Checking customer's credit ratings with banks*
- *Negotiating re-payment plans*
- *Dealing with internal queries about payments*

Salary: The starting salary for a credit controller can range between £17,000 and £28,000 per year but this can rise to over £45,000 plus if you move up the ladder to become a credit control manager.

vi. Tax Adviser

Job profile: As a tax adviser you will provide a professional advisory and consultancy service to clients, interpret complicated tax legislation (and it's implications to the client) and plan the best strategy to plan clients financial affairs and minimise future tax liabilities.

You could work for an accountancy firm, a specialist tax consultancy or a company with its own tax team. Banks, legal firms and HM Revenue and Customs also need good tax specialists.

You could also choose to become a freelance tax consultant and start your own business. Why not?

The typical duties to perform in this role will include but not limited to:

- *Researching and understanding tax law*
- *Liaising with HM Revenue and Customs on your clients' behalf*
- *Checking and completing tax forms*
- *Meeting clients to gather information and explain options available to them*
- *Auditing clients' tax records*

Individuals, small businesses and large companies all need good, clear and simple tax advice. So your job is really a very important one and one you should cherish.

Salary: Starting salary of Tax Adviser is at £20,000-£37,000 rising to £30,000-£55,000 upon obtaining the ATT qualification (ATT) or even £65,000 plus with the CTA qualification and substantial experience.

vii. Payroll Administrator

Job profile: You'll be involved with creating new payroll policies and procedures, reporting back to the management team and ensuring all the computer systems are up to date in terms of government legislation like RTI, pensions etc.

As part of the payroll administration team the duties that you will perform include but are not limited to the following:

- *Checking people's hours*
- *Making the weekly or monthly salary/wage payments on time*
- *Issuing payslips to employees*
- *Working out tax and national insurance deductions*
- *Submitting the payroll report to HMRC*
- *Providing the accountants with the payroll journal figures to be posted into the accounts*
- *Setting up new members of staff on the payroll*
- *Calculating overtime*

- *Issuing tax forms (P45s, P60, etc.)*

- *Managing special situations like maternity or sickness, holiday*

You could work as part of the payroll team in an organisation or for a payroll bureau - a company that specialises in running the payroll for other companies.

Average salary: If you're just starting out as a payroll administrator you should be on £13,000 to £18,000 a year. This jumps up to £20,000 and £25,000 as you get more qualified and more experienced.

viii. Finance Manager

Job profile: As a finance manager you'll work with all departments of the business to help them plan and manage their budgets. You'll also work closely with the CEO to help him/her manage the overall business so it makes the most money it can.

Where you work will have an impact on the work you do. In a bigger company the role is often more strategic and involves a lot of analysis and you might be the finance director for a division rather than for the whole company. If you work for a smaller company you'll probably have to be a bit more hands on with general accounts matters too.

It's a broad and interesting role covering activities like:

- *Monitoring cash flow*

- *Supervising your own accounts team*

- *Monitoring business performance*

- *Developing financial models*

- *Preparing accounts*

- *Overseeing the budgets and that everyone is sticking to them*

- *Working with departments and teams*

- *Planning for the future*

- *Competitor analysis*

- *Strategic planning*

Average salary: £53,660 (GMB/ONS)

ix. Management Accountant

Job profile: Management accountants look to the future rather than the past when assessing the financial status of an organisation. Their role is to provide the financial information necessary to enable an organisation's management team to make sound strategic decisions.

Some organisations will have their own management accountants. You could also work for a private accountancy firm which offers accountancy services to fee-paying clients.

The kind of activities you'll oversee include:

- *Making sure spending is in line with budgets*

- *Recommending ways of cutting costs*

- *Analysing your company's financial performance and making longer term forecasts*

- *Providing information for audits*
- *Working with all departments and the management team to help make financial decisions*

A big focus of your job will be to make sure the business is compliant with financial governance requirements.

You'll most likely manage a team who will help you with all your duties although the role does vary quite widely depending on the size of the business and what sector it is in.

Average salary: Typical starting salary is £21,000, £30,000-£45,000 with experience rising to £60,000+ for senior position (CIMA)

x. Auditor

Job profile: As an auditor your job is to ensure that an organisation is using its resources in the most efficient ways – whether for the sake of the taxpayer in the public sector, or shareholders in private businesses.

You are responsible for auditing the accounts of an organisation, analysing expenditure and its effectiveness, assessing risks to financial control and accountability.

You'll not only have to write reports on your findings, but you may also find yourself in a boardroom giving PowerPoint presentations to managers and directors. You'll be expected to keep on top of the many – many – changes in the law and keep a rational view of the best way ahead when all around you people are flapping in a panic.

You will in many instances need strong communication skills, lots of tact, and confidence in your own ability.

Average salary: On a graduate trainee scheme straight out of college, your starting salary will be £18,000-£22,000 a year. Once you're fully-fledged, an auditor can expect to earn £35,000-£45,000 in a public sector position, rising to well over £60,000 as a senior audit manager. £49,072 - £63,235 is the average according to National Audit Office.

Well, in many cases, a progressive career in accountancy requires that you have sufficient work experience. If you need to gain UK work experience in accountancy, TD&A certified accountants may be able to help you. Visit their website at: http://tdanda.co.uk/careers/

Now having listed all of the above top 10 jobs you could choose as a career path in accounting, let's look at some of the key strategies and principles that can help you secure one of the above mentioned jobs.

Top tips on how to get accounting jobs

The Top five things you should put on your CV

- *The CV needs to be relevant to your Job/company*
- *Show you have a range of experience*
- *Clearly state your qualifications*
- *Show you can respond to challenges*
- *Detail your achievements*

Qualifications like ACCA, CIMA, AAT, ICAEW will arm you with the knowledge and skills that project solid technical and professional capabilities.

When applying for roles, you need to find out where your strengths lie and what really interests you when applying for roles.

Take some time to do some work experience within a finance department and gain solid relevant practical work experience in accountancy.

The Top five things to do during an interview

If you are successful in a job application and you are called for an interview, here are top five things you should do during your interview:

- *Be honest – don't try to make up an answer if you don't know something.*
- *Show evidence of your competencies.*
- *Communicate clearly – eye contact, answering questions fully, using appropriate language are all important.*
- *Show passion for the company.*
- *Be professional.*

Besides knowing what you should do at interviews, you should also know what you should not do at interviews. Here they are:

- *Don't rush into giving an answer or response to a question, ensure you understand what's being asked and consider the context of the question.*
- *Do not go unprepared and make sure you have thought about the sort of questions you might be asked and have examples for each question.*

- *Refrain from using technical jargon where possible and talk about your contribution to a task, not just what your opinion or point of view on the subject.*

How your tax code is worked out

Everyone who works in the UK somehow pays tax and the amount of tax you pay is calculated based on the tax code that you have been given by HMRC.

It would be interesting to find out how your tax code is worked out. Wouldn't it? Well, here are the steps:

Step one
Your tax allowances are added up. (In most cases this will just be your Personal allowance and any blind person's allowance. However in some cases it may include certain job expenses.)

Step two
Income you've not paid tax on (for example untaxed interest or part-time earnings) and any taxable employment benefits are added up.

Step three
The total amount of income you've not paid any tax on (called 'deductions') is taken away from the total amount of tax allowances. The amount you are left with is the total of tax-free income you are allowed in a tax year.

Step four

Broadly speaking, to arrive at your tax code the amount of tax-free income you are left with is divided by 10 and added to the letter which fits your circumstances.

For example, the tax code 117L means:

- *you are entitled to the basic Personal Allowance of £1,170 which has to be taken away from your total taxable income and you pay tax on what's left*

The tax code spreads your tax-free amount equally over the year so that you get about the same take-home pay or pension each week or month.

That's it.

Now, next time you receive a coding notice from HMRC, you will look at your tax code and know exactly how they worked it out.

GETTING STARTED WELL

The code of professional ethics

What you ought to realise as you start your practical accounting career is that, the distinguishing feature of the accountancy profession is its acceptance of the responsibility to act in the public interest, hence your responsibility as an accountant is not exclusively to satisfy the needs of an individual client or employer. In acting in the public interest therefore, you shall observe and comply with the code of professional ethics.

Here are they:

i. **Integrity**: *You have to be straightforward and honest in all professional relationships*

ii. **Objectivity**: *You are not to allow bias, conflict of interest or undue influence of others to overide professional or business judgements at any time.*

iii. **Confidentiality**: *respect the confidentiality of information acquired as a result of professional and business relationships and not to disclose any such information to third parties without proper and specific authority unless there is a legal or professional right or duty to disclose. Confidential information acquired as a result of professional and business relationships shall not be for your personal advantage or third parties.*

iv. **Professional competence & due care**: *As a professional accountant,* *you are to maintain professional knowledge and skill at the level required to ensure that a client or employer receives competent professional service based on current developments in practice, legislation and techniques. You shall act diligently and in accordance with applicable technical and professional standards when providing professional services.*

v. **Adopt professional behaviour** *to comply with relevant laws and regulations and avoid any action that brings the accounting profession into disrepute.*

The fundamental basics you need to know

As you start your accounting career, here are 10 fundamental basic things ranging from those directly concerned with the organisation you will be working in to the general accounting & business principles.

1. *The nature of the business & business structure in use.*

2. *What a financial document is*

3. *Double entry system (PEA.RL)*

4. *The accounting equation: Assets = Liabilities + Owner's Equity*

5. *Working with HMRC & commom business taxes*

6. *Difference between tax year & financial year*

7. *The importance of working to deadlines*

8. *Having good computer typing speed.*

9. *How to use some accounting/bookkeeping software*

10. *Key stages in practical accounting.*

Let's briefly look at each of the above 10 things.

The nature of the business and the business structure in use or in place.

Here, the nature of the business is essentially what the business does in terms of its trade e.g. an accounting firm, a retail business etc. The business structure in use would be a sole trader, partnership, limited company or charity.

It is important for you to understand the above at the very onset of your

work experience because you will be in a better position to understand the cost & revenue base of the business in a much better way and you will find that doing the accounts of that business later will be a lot more straight forward than if you were not so much aware of the facts regarding the nature of the business & its structure.

What a financial document is

Here we are looking at things like invoices, credit notes, receipts, statements, contracts etc. Basically any document that has an impact or effect on the financial position of a business is a financial document.

Financial documents are later processed to form a set of transaction data that will eventually be used to produce accounting reports for management and for external purposes.

Double entry system

I know you have dealt with this a lot in your theoretical studies but its application is even more relevant now that you are in practice. I will talk about this a little later but for now, suffice it to say that in a double-entry accounting system, every transaction affects at least two of your accounts, so you make at least two entries – hence the name – double entry.

Remember, many computerised accounting systems make this process easy and is automatically done for you by the software.

The financial condition of every business is described by the accounting equation Assets = Liabilities + Owners Equity, and there are only two possible ways that the items in the equation can change: either they can increase or decrease. An accounting system therefore is simply a way of recording increases and decreases. There are a number of bookkeeping accounting systems/softwares: Sage 50 Accounts, Quickbooks, TAS, Iris, VT etc. Each of them will help you record accounting transactions correctly if you know how to use them.

Bookkeeping is a relatively straightforward endeavour once you know how to use any of the accounting systems and get in the habit of staying on top of entries. It is simply a matter of tracking funds flowing into and out of your business, and allocating these funds to appropriate categories. By performing basic bookkeeping tasks regularly, you master the essentials and avoid the hassle of tasks piling up and becoming intimidating. We will talk about this a little later.

Working with HMRC and common business taxes.

I don't mean here that you literally have to work with HMRC like your other member of staff. No, not like that.

What I mean here is that, when you start working in any organisation, it would be good for you to know where the tax office of that organisation is, what kind of taxes the business pays to HMRC (PAYE, VAT, NI, Stamp duty, etc.), know the contact telephone number for the tax office and various other help and guidance from HMRC for the business in the industry where the business you work for is.

Difference between a tax year and a financial year

In the UK a tax year is fixed and is from 6th April current year to the following 5th April next year and a financial year basically starts when a business starts trading. This will become very relevant if you have different rates of corporation tax each tax year and a business happens to have a financial year that straddles two tax years. You will have to apportion the profits accordingly using the different rates of tax to calculate the corporation tax due.

The importance of working to deadlines

In accounting, there are many deadlines you have to meet during your work (filing of accounts, tax returns, management reports, investment appraisal reports etc.) and failure to do so can result to serious consequences like fines and even being sacked. It is therefore very important that you understand what deadlines you have to meet when you start work and make sure that you deliver within the deadlines if you desire a long and rewarding career in accounting.

Having good computer typing speed

The "tech" world of accounting nowadays means that keyboards are an essential part of your work and your typing speed will, to a large extent, determine how fast you complete your tasks.

So, if you are not very good at typing, invest in some speed typing course or you can practice with typing tests online and get yourself on to the fast track of having a reputation for great typing speed. It will serve you well.

How to use some bookkeeping/accounting software

A lot of accounting procedures nowadays are so computerised and having knowledge of how to use one or more of the accounting/bookkeeping software's out there can dramatically improve your employability and chances of career progression.

You should at least know how to use any of the following: Sage 50 accounts, QuickBooks, Iris, VT, Xero, exact online, etc. Some of these have desk top versions as well as cloud versions but things seem to be heading more to cloud accounting and you should learn how to use both the desktop and cloud version of whichever software you choose.

THE KEY STAGES IN PRACTICAL ACCOUNTING

There are three key stages in accounting: Analysis, Processing & Reporting. I call them "APR" for short. See figure below.

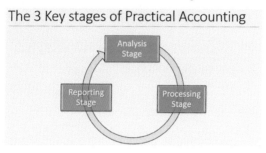

Fig. 1

In each stage, there are 3 distinct things that you will need to do. Let's look at each of them.

1ˢᵗ stage: - Analysis

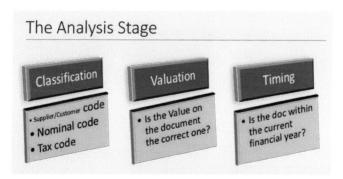

Fig. 2

You see, operations of a business can be quite complex, involving marketing, finance, production, research and development and acomplex flow of resources in and out of the business. All of this result in generation of financial documents.

These financial documents could be invoices, credit notes, receipts, contracts, bank statements, supplier statements etc.

Therefore, when it comes to working in accounting, it is very important that the financial documents are properly analysed before the are processed or recorded in the ledgers.

The way these financial documents are analysed is by doing three things as illustrated in the figure above: classification, valuation & timing.

Let's look at how each of them is done.

i. Classification

Classifying a document means to code it. There are three main codes you will be working with or using every time you classify a document. They are:

- *The supplier/customer code*
- *The nominal code*
- *The Tax code*

A customer/supplier code is a code you use to identify your customers or suppliers in your records. Each customer & supplier will have their own unique account code for easy reference. For example BOC001 as an account code for Blue Ocean Cruisers Ltd

Depending on the bookkeeping or accounting software in use in your organisation, the nominal code is used to allocate or identify the category of the ledger account, either in the balance sheet or profit and loss account that the transaction in the financial document should be recorded under.

For example, if you receive an invoice from British Gas for your gas bill, you could classify it by writing down the nominal code for gas (e.g 7205) if you are using Sage 50 Accounts for example.

A tax code is a code used to identify the VAT rate to be used when processing the document in the ledgers. There are different rates of VAT and each code will represent a rate. For example, in Sage 50 accounts, T1 is the standard rated tax code - 20% VAT, T0 for 0% VAT, T9 is a VAT code for transactions that are outside the scope of VAT.

If you are working in an organisation with many departments, you could also have a department code.

ii. Valuation

Valuing a document means ascertaining whether the currency values (e.g £ or $ values) showing on the document are correct.

If an invoice from one of your suppliers is for example showing a value of £5,000 you will need to verify this figure by crosschecking it with goods received notes (GRN's), Local purchase orders (LPO's) and also get a signed acknowledgement from the the person who placed the order for the goods or services.

iii. Timing

Timing means making sure that the document(s) to be recorded or processed relates to the financial period you are working with. For example, you should not post an invoice relating to next accounting period into the current accounting period and vice versa.

2nd Stage: Processing stage

After your analysis, here are two things to take into consideration before you record/process the data.

✓ *The data to be recorded must be reliable. This means that the transaction data can be verified as authentic and that the data is unbiased.*

✓ *The data must be relevant. This means that the data will provide information that is useful and significant. It should not be irrelevant or imaterial. Reliable and relevant data will ultimately result in reliable and relevant information in financial reports.*

The following tasks are performed at the processing stage:

Fig. 3

Lets look at what is done at each task:

i. Data entry

The main activity that happens during this task is input of invoice records (customer & supplier), receipts & credit notes on to the accounting ledgers after doing the analysis.

ii. Administration

The main activities that happen during the administrative task at the processing stage are:

- *Providing clerical & administrative support to management*
- *Banking receipts from customers & cash sales*
- *Paying suppliers & reconciling supplier statements*
- *Managing petty cash*
- *Sorting out post, both physical and electronic (email)*
- *Doing bank & account reconciliations*
- *Preparing & submitting VAT returns to HMRC*
- *Answering phones & ordering office stationary*

iii. Debtor management

Collecting outstanding debts from debtors and making sure that bad debts are minimised or completely eliminated is the main activity here.

Here is the summary of the processing stage tasks:

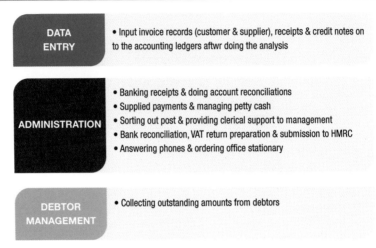

Fig. 4

3rd Stage: Reporting stage

After you have analysed and processed the financial documents as stated in the first two stages (analysis & processing stages), there will be a lot of transaction data available to produce reports. Hence the third stage – reporting stage

The key aspect of this stage is *summarisation*.

Summarisation here means accumulating and organising data in ways that make the recorded data more understandable and useful. Proper summarising makes it possible to present data in financial reports. When summarisisation happens, the data can be transformed into useful and usable information.

One example of summarised data is a Trial balance – a list of balances of the ledger accounts

There are three things that happen at this stage, let's have a look at them.

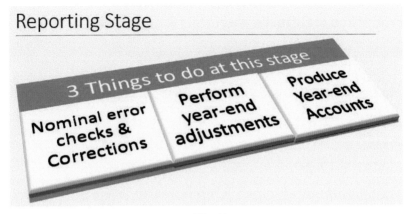

Fig. 5

Let us briefly look at the three things to be done at this stage

i. Nominal error checks and corrections

What you will do here will mostly include the following:

- *Produce a trial balance*
- *Check each nominal account in the trial balance for any errors*
- *Make necessary corrections (you can use journals) and update the nominal accounts*

ii. Yearend account adjustments

The adjustments and reconciliations that need to be done at this point are:

- *Accruals & Prepayments*
- *Depreciation & calculating capital allowances*
- *Bank Reconciliation*

- *Control Accounts Reconciliations (Debtors, Creditors, VAT, Wages)*

iii. Production of financial statements & tax returns

During this task, you basically do the following:

- *Produce financial reports (SOCI/P&L, SOFP/Balance sheet, Cash flow statement)*
- *Prepare a Corporation Tax Return (CT600) or Personal Tax Return (SA100) & Computations and file them with HMRC*
- *Prepare abridged accounts and file them with companies house*

Let's look at the summary of what happens in the reporting stage;

Nominal Error Checks & Corrections	• Produce a trial balance • Check each nominal account in the trial balance for trial balance errors • Make necessary corrections (you can use journals)
Yearend Account Adjustments	• Accruals & Prepayments • Depreciation & capital allowances calculations • Bank Reconciliation • Control Accounts Reconciliations (Debtors, Creditors, VAT, Wages)
Production Of Financial Statements & Tax Returns	• Produce financial reports (SOCI/P&L, SOFP/Balance sheet, Cash flow statement) • Prepare a Corporation Tax Return (CT600) or Personal Tax Return (SA100) & Computations and file them with HMRC • Prepare abridged accounts and file them with companies house.

Fig. 6

So, what we have just been saying is this; fundamentally, practical accounting is done in three key stages:

- *Analysis - of business financial documents*
- *Processing – of business financial transactions in the financial documents*
- *Reporting – on the financial position of the business*

Now, let's summarise what we have been talking about in a simple diagram that we'll call the accounting cycle wheel.

The Accounting cycle wheel

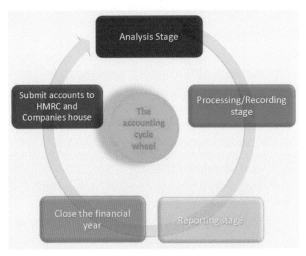

Fig. 6

Looking at the figure above, you start by analysing the financial documents by coding them with supplier & customer codes where applicable, nominal codes to identify the nature of the transaction, and tax codes to reflect the correct treatment of VAT in the financial document.

You then have to process all of the financial documents that have been analysed by inputing them into the computerised accounting software being used in the organisation.

You might at this point also receive money owed from debtors as well as pay suppliers and do adhog accounting administration tasks including reconciliations, petty cash management and VAT return preparation and submission to HMRC

After successfully inputing all the financial documents into the accounting software, there will be a database of financial transactions formed that the manager will now use to produce financial reports - hence the reporting stage.

But before the manager proceeds to produce the financial reports {statement of comprehensive income (the profit & loss account), the statement of financial position (balance sheet) and cash flow statement} , he/she would have to first check for any errors in the nominal accounts and correct them.

He/she will then do yearend adjustments including accrual and prepayment adjustments, depreciation and capital allowances calculations and control account reconciliations (debtors, creditors, Wages, VAT etc)

Once the annual accounts are finanlised and approved, the manager can then close the financial year and submit the returns and accounts to HMRC & companies house - the CT600 for small to medium sized companies and the abridged accounts.

There you go, not very complicated, is it? No.

Now you know what the accounting cycle looks like, don't you?

APPLICATION OF ACCOUNTING THEORY IN PRACTICE

I hope the introduction to practical aspects of accounting as stated above inspired you as they have for many of the trainees that I have had the awesome privilege of mentoring and training over the years.

What I would like to do now is to have a look at some of the fundamental basics of accounting theory and show you how you can apply them in practice during the course of your career.

The accounting equation

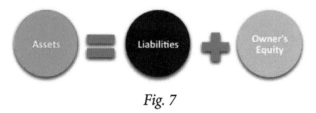

Fig. 7

The equation above is the foundation of double entry accounting.

This accounting equation displays that all assets are either financed by borrowing money or paying with the money of the company's shareholders/business owner(s).

The equation is generally written with liabilities appearing before owner's equity because creditors usually have to be repaid before investors in a bankruptcy. In this sense, the liabilities are considered more current than the equity. This is consistent with financial reporting where current assets and liabilities are always reported before long-term assets and liabilities.

The accounting equation is also written as Liabilities = Assets – Owners Equity and Owners Equity = Assets – Liabilities.

The balance sheet is a complex display of this equation, showing that the total assets of a company are equal to the total of liabilities and shareholder/owners' equity. Any purchase or sale has an equal effect on both sides of the equation, or offsetting effects on the same side of the equation.

When later doing your balance sheet reconciliation, you have to take the above facts in to consideration.

For businesses, it is vital for balance sheets to be reconciled at the end of an accounting period.

Balance sheet reconciliation is part of the accounting period closing process and it is important because it helps to identify any errors before closing. You would be absolutely right in saying that balance sheet reconciliations are one method of making sure account information is accurate and thorough. What you will be doing is to ensure that there are no mistakes in the information for the purpose of records and for management decision making.

When an account is reconciled on a balance sheet, several different detailed ledgers are utilised. Cash accounts are generally reconciled against bank statements, and accounts payable and accounts receivable are usually reconciled against ageing schedules. Both fixed assets and inventories are reconciled against physical counts.

Application of double entry principle

Getting a grasp on double entry and using journals when working with a accounting softwares has been quite challange for many of the trainees I have worked with.

Here are some facts and guidelines to help you understnad this concept in practice.

- *You will always use both a debit and a credit for every journal entry - it is what the system of double-entry bookkeeping is based on. You have two columns in your journal entry. Each will have an equal entry - one for a debit, one for a credit.*

It is like T accounts; if one account is debited, the other account will have a corresponding credit entry

- *Remember the format of the Accounting Equation where Assets = Liabilities + Owners Equity. The Asset side is the left side of the equation and the Liabilities + Owner's Equity is the right side of the equation.*

When you need to make a journal entry, refer to your Chart of Accounts to see if the account you need to use falls on the left or right side of the accounting equation.

- *If the account is on the Asset or left side, it is the Debit side (the accounts on the right side are usually purchase, asset and expense accounts). A debit will increase those accounts and a credit will decrease them. If the account is on the Liabilities and Owner's Equity or right side, it is the Credit side (the accounts on the right side are usually revenue, liabilities & the capital account). A credit will increase those accounts and a debit will decrease them.*

Let me illustrate what I have just been saying using the PEARL acronym

P	PURCHASES	These have Debit balances in the ledgers	They increase by debit entries and decrease by Credit entries
E	EXPENSES		
A	ASSETS		
R	REVENUE	These have Credit balances in the ledgers	They increase by Credit entries and decrease by Debit entries
L	LIABILITIES		

Here is the double entry principle in a nutshell – see figure below

For every Debit Entry

There is an equal & coresponding credit entry

Fig. 8

Sales ledger process

Fig. 9

Your company's most vital asset is its customers. Without them, you would not, and could not, exist in business. You need to treat your customers well but also ensure that the customers pay on time to avoid cash flow issues as already mentioned in this book.

Here is then how to make sure your customers pay on time:

- *Make sure you invoice your existing customers regularly. It's all too easy to focus on the job and delay the paperwork. But the sooner you get your invoices out, the sooner you'll get your payments in.*

- *Be clear about your payment terms. Always ensure your invoices are dated, with clear statements of the amount due and your payment terms – for example "payment due within 30 days".*

- *Make them an offer they can't refuse. If it's important to get cash back into your business quickly, why not think about offering discounts to customers who pay upfront or early?*

- *Accept card payments. You'll get paid quickly and if your customers use a credit card they could benefit from up to 56 days interest-free credit before they need to make a payment.*

Purchase ledger process

Fig. 10

Features of a valid supplier invoice	
Address details	Invoices must be addressed to the business or department within the organisation. The name of an individual may appear in addition as long as this is an authorised signatory.
Status of document	The document must be an invoice rather than a delivery note, order acknowledgement or statement. Some invoices from smaller suppliers may not contain all of the details for VAT purposes. If the word 'invoice' appears on the document then it should be treated as an invoice.
Accurate	The currency value in the document should be arithmetically correct.

VAT invoice	Invoices that charge VAT must contain all of the following details in addition to those given above: • *Supplier VAT number;* • *Supplier's trading name and address;* • *Description of goods or services;* • *Invoice number;* • *Invoice date;* • *Time of supply - 'tax point' if different from the invoice date;* • *Analysis of VAT charged, including value and rate used.*

DAY-TO-DAY TASKS EARLY IN YOUR ACCOUNTING CAREER

Now let's look at some of the common tasks you will be in doing especially at the early stages of your career.

Let's start by looking at;

Data entry

In accounting data entry (or database administration), it's often the case that you will update and maintain information on computer systems and in archives.

It's an important role as information in these systems is only valuable if it is accurate, up to date and useable.

This task is quite straightforward and your day will involve entering information into the computerised database. The type of information varies and it could be sales data or personal information on new clients, purchase data or personal information on new suppliers.

Information you work with might be text based or numerical. It could be paper-based information like the information on financial documents that needs logging into spreadsheets or databases or accounting software.

The next task we will look at is that of;

Debtor management

Debtor management is very important because it has a significant impact on cash flow. In business, cash flow is key to business success and survival.

Although late-paying customers can be a hazard for any business, there are plenty of ways you can reduce the risks of those customers becoming bad debtors and it is done through excellent debtor management – part of credit control.

Here is how it works:

- *Get a current aged debtors list from the records/accounting system.*
- *Review all debts which are considered overdue.*
- *Send customer a current statement or gentle reminder.*
- *5 working days after sending the statement check to see whether the account has been paid.*
- *If it is not paid print debt collection record sheet.*
- *Telephone the client and discuss the reason for non-payment, remind them of their credit terms, and agree a payment date.*
- *Write a letter to the client summarising the telephone conversation and noting the agreed payment date.*
- *Make a note on the system of the date payment should be received.*
- *If payment is not received by the agreed date telephone the client and remind them of your previous discussion.*

- *Agree a date for payment (or standing order/credit card if applicable).*

- *Write a letter to the client summarising the telephone conversation and noting the agreed payment date.*

- *Make a note on the system of the date payment should be received.*

- *If payment is not received by the agreed date telephone the client.*

- *Write a letter to the client summarising the telephone conversation and noting the date court proceedings will commence.*

- *Make a note on the system of the date payment should be received.*

- *If payment is not received within the specified time then continue with the County Court procedure:*

  » *Complete Form N1 (claim form).*

  » *You must also ensure that the back of this form is completed.*

  » *Calculate the interest due.*

  » *Calculate the fee - this will depend on the amount you are claiming.*

  » *Take photocopies of the completed Form N1.*

  » *Send form N1, the copies for the Court and the defendants and a cheque for the court fee to the County Court.*

Receiving money from debtors

If you are going to receive payment from debtors or cash paying customers by using a chip & pin credit card machine follow the following steps

1 Make sure that the credit card machine is 'Ready'.

2 Enter the amount being paid and confirm the amount is correct, press enter and hand the machine to the customer to insert their card and enter their PIN.

3 The receipt should print after the customer enters their correct pin

4 Take the receipt and the card and hand the card back to the customer. If the first receipt reads card holder copy hand it over to the customer as well.

5 Press enter again on the card machine and a second receipt will print. If the first receipt was cardholders copy, the second receipt will be merchant copy.

6 Attach the merchant copy to the back of the daily income sheet and enter the details in the income sheet.

Fig. 11

When the customer authorises payment by credit/debit card over the phone follow the following steps:

- *Get the customer information over the phone. You need the customer's credit/debit card number, card expiration date, billing address, security code (number from back of card) and amount of purchase. Ask the customer if they would like their receipt mailed or emailed to them, then get the appropriate address. Always get the customer's phone number as you may need to call back.*

- *Enter the information into the card terminal. This may vary slightly depending on your terminal, but most have a similar process. Push the "sale" button on your terminal. The first prompt usually offers two options: card present or sale by phone. You will choose "sale by phone." Then follow the prompts, filling in the customer information and confirming the sale amount.*

- *Complete the transaction. Confirm the information and push "enter" for the last prompt. Terminal will display "transaction complete" or similar notification. If there is an option to "print receipt," push "yes." Some terminals will automatically print out two receipts when the transaction is complete. Just be sure you have a merchant copy and a customer copy. The customer receipt may display a sentence that says, "Phone order" or similar, instead of a signature line. If the customer receipt does not say "phone order," write this on the receipt.*

- *Mail the client's receipt. Scan and email the phone payment receipt or send it through the post to your customer. It is best practice to take the opportunity to thank the client for their business every time you send a correspondence.*

After taking payment as stated above, do the following:

- *Enter any other income onto the Daily Income sheet.*

- *At the end of the day produce a daily report for card machine transactions and enter the details onto the income sheet as 'Credit/ debit card banked'.*

- *Remove the amount to be banked and put into the safe with the paying-in slip for banking the following day.*

- *Complete a paying-in slip for the banking and enter the total to be banked onto the daily income sheet.*

- *Make sure that each individual receipt is clearly described on the paying in slip showing who it is from and if known the invoice number it relates to.*

Dealing with petty cash

Another aspect of your role as you start your career in accounting is dealing with petty cash entries.

The objective of the petty cash management is to ensure that control is kept over the petty cash tin and that all cash payments are recorded correctly and entered onto the accounting system.

Businesses generally keep small amounts of cash to meet small miscellaneous payments such as entertainment expenses and stationery costs. Such payments are generally handled by a petty cash imprest system whereby an amount of 'Float' is fixed (say £250). This is the maximum amount of cash that can be held at any time and each time cash level runs low, the petty cash imprest is injected with cash by drawing a cheque.

The amount of reimbursement is equal to the expenses paid through petty cash since the time of last reimbursement. Petty cash balance after reimbursement reverts to back to the level of the float (in this case £250).

For security reasons, the petty cash fund should be locked at all times when it is not in use. Access to petty cash tin is restricted and money cannot be taken out of it without approval.

Any money taken from the petty cash tin should be replaced with a petty cash voucher. This states what the money was taken for and who took it. The voucher should be signed by the financial accountant or designated signatory.

Whenever a voucher is completed, it is good practice for the custodian to immediately update the petty cash book by adding the amount, type, and date of the expenditure and updating the running cash balance.

For example, if you got some refreshments for the office, e.g. some sweets and you need to be reimbursed the amount you spent, you would need to fill out a petty cash voucher as below.

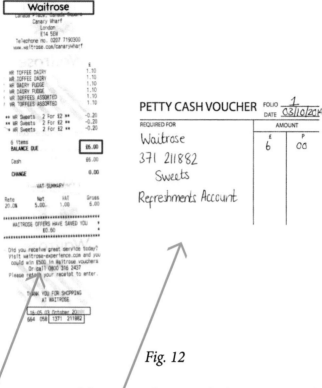

Fig. 12

If a receipt is received for a purchase made from petty cash then this should be attached to the petty cash voucher.

The total of the petty cash vouchers and the actual cash in the tin should always add up to the agreed cash float amount (e.g. £250). You will then need to fill this information onto your Petty Cash report on Excel as shown below

PETTY CASH REPORT

COMPANY NAME:	Example Ltd				BALANCE B/F		£250	

REPORTING PERIOD: FROM 03/10/2015 TO 03/10/2015

Date	voucher No.	Refference	Description	Account	Cash in	Cash out	Balance
03/10/2015	1	waitrose 131211	Sweets	Refreshments		£6.00	£244.00
							£0.00
							£0.00
							£0.00
							£0.00
							£0.00
							£0.00
							£0.00
							£0.00
							£0.00
							£0.00
							£0.00
							£0.00
							£0.00
Total						£6.00	

CHECKED &	Total spent	£6.00
APPROVED	Amount needed to top up float	£244.00
BY:	TOTAL FLOAT AMOUNT	£250.00

Each week the petty cash vouchers should be recorded on a report then added up and a cheque cashed for that amount. This cash should be put back into the petty cash tin, so that the cash in the tin is brought back up to the agreed maximum amount

Petty cash funds should only be disbursed for minor business expenses and every disbursement request should be screened. A petty cash voucher should be completed by the person who requires reimbursement of expenses. This voucher should contain the amount to be disbursed, the type of expense, the date, and the person to whom the petty cash is to be paid. If there is a receipt for which the person is being reimbursed, staple it to the voucher. This step is needed to track the types of expenditures being made, which can then be charged to various expense accounts.

To get a reimbursement for the float, a petty cash reconciliation form has to be completed, in which the petty cash custodian lists the remaining cash on hand, vouchers issued, and any overage or underage. The voucher information may come from the petty cash book. An accounting staff person reviews and approves the form and sends a copy to the accounts payable staff, along with all vouchers referenced on the form. The petty cash custodian retains a copy.

VAT Returns

During the early and even late stages of your accounting career, you will be required to produce, reconcile and submit VAT returns to HMRC if the organisation you are working for is VAT registered.

So, here is a VAT return procedure to get you started.

To begin with, note that there is a 5 –step process of completing a VAT return and every VAT return you process should be submitted to HMRC on time every tax period.

A tax period for VAT is usually three months. Any payment of VAT that is due should reach HMRC by the due date, which should be shown on the online VAT return and online VAT return acknowledgement.

The 5 – step process is as stated below:

1. *Gather together your business records for the tax period*
2. *Use the business records to create your VAT account for the period and from your records, establish:*

a. *VAT due in the period on sales and other outputs*

b. *VAT due in the period on acquisitions from other EC (European Community) member states*

c. *VAT reclaimed in the period on purchases and other inputs (including acquisitions from the EC)*

d. *Total Value of sales and all other outputs excluding any VAT*

e. *Total value of purchases and all other inputs excluding any VAT*

f. *Total value of all supplies of goods and related costs, excluding any VAT, to other EC member states*

g. *Total Value of acquisitions of goods and related costs excluding any VAT, from EC member states*

3. *Once you have established the figures in 2 a-g above, use them to fill the VAT return online form*

4. *Review the online form to make sure that all the entries are correct*

5. *Submit the VAT return electronically online and reconcile the VAT return in your accounting system. Remember to make arrangement to pay any VAT due (if applicable) as soon as possible. If you are due a repayment from HM Excise and Customs, a payment will be sent to you.*

I have written a book titled "Get your VAT return done in 5 steps"

and it gives you detailed guidance and screen shots of how to prepare, reconcile and submit your VAT return. If you would like a copy, get it at www.sterlinglibs.com.

Anyway, back to VAT....

VAT Return checklist

Step	Description	Tick
i	Has all output tax been traced to sales invoices or Daily Income sheets and invoices?	
ii	Has all output tax been declared at the correct VAT rate?	
iii	Has all input tax been traced to purchase invoices and petty cash vouchers?	
iv	Has all input tax been claimed at the correct VAT rate?	
v	Have all bank receipt and bank payment entries been checked to ensure that the correct VAT code has been applied?	
vi	Have all bad debts been entered onto the accounting system and the VAT claimed?	
vii	Have sales invoices been issued for any asset sales? Has the correct output tax been declared?	
viii	Check that no input tax has been claimed for goods for private use	
ix	Check that input tax has not been claimed for entertainment (unless it can be proven to be wholly and exclusively a business cost)	
x	Has a fuel scale charge been included in the VAT calculation (needed if the company pays ANY private petrol/diesel bills)?	
xi	Has only 50% of the input VAT been claimed on any cars that are leased or hired?	
xii	If you make exempt supplies have you checked whether the partial exemption rules apply?	
xiii	If you import or export goods have all the documentation been kept and recorded and treated correctly for VAT purposes?	
xiv	If you have dealt with firms in other countries have you recorded their VAT registration numbers?	
xv	Has the nominal code for VAT been checked to ensure that no journals have been entered which would affect the VAT return?	
xvi	Have all manual additions been checked?	

Bank Reconciliation

Another aspect of your role in your early years of your accounting career and even later is doing bank reconciliations.

You see, a company's cash balance at bank and its cash balance according to its accounting records usually do not match. This is due to the fact that, at any particular date, cheques may be outstanding, deposits may be in transit to the bank, errors may have occurred etc.

Therefore companies have to carry out bank reconciliation process which prepares a statement accounting for the difference between the cash balance in company's cash account and the cash balance according to its bank statement.

The benefit of reconciling the bank statement is knowing that the amount of Cash reported by the company (company's books) is consistent with the amount of cash shown in the bank's records.

When the company receives its bank statement, the company should verify that the amounts on the bank statement are consistent or compatible with the amounts in the company's cash account in its general ledger and vice versa.

The causes of disagreements between the bank balance & the cash book balance in the general ledger are:

In the bank statement

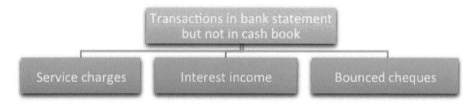

Fig. 13

In the cash book

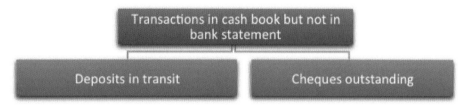

Fig. 14

Here is a bank reconciliation report template.

ABC Company Ltd.
Bank Reconciliation (Current Account)
For the Year Ended ....

	£
Balance per cash account in general ledger	
Adjustments to cash account (based on bank statement):	
Add: Bank interest	
Credit / wire transfers	
Subtract: Bank charges	
Standing orders	
Direct debits	
Dishonoured cheques	
Add/Subtract: Errors	
Adjusted cash account in general ledger	-
Balance per bank statement	
Adjustments to bank statement balance (based on accounting records):	
Add: Deposits in transit	
Subtract: Cheques issued, but have not cleared bank	
Add/Subtract: Bank errors	
Adjusted balance per bank statement	-
Adjusted cash account in general ledger	-
Adjusted balance per bank statement	-
Difference	-
Reconciling items	
1	
2	
3	
Total reconciling items (= Difference)	-

Okay, so far we have looked at some of the key duties you are most likely to do at the early stages of your accounting career. There are also some administrative duties you will be required to perform.

Ad hog administrative duties

Here are some common administrative duties that you will from time to time be involved in doing.

1. Sorting incoming post

Objective: To make sure that incoming mail is dealt with in a secure and controlled way.

a. *When mail is received, open envelopes addressed to the company*

b. *Envelopes addressed to individual people within the company and marked as 'private and confidential' should be passed to them.*

c. *Once mail is opened it should be date stamped, and distributed to the relevant people.*

d. *If a courier arrives with a parcel, it should be checked for obvious damages and signed for.*

e. *The parcel should then be passed onto the relevant person.*

f. *If it is not addressed to anyone specific it should be opened and the contents checked to the delivery note attached to the parcel.*

h. *If the contents do not agree to the delivery note or are damaged in any way, contact the sender and advise them.*

i. *If the contents are as stated on the delivery note, the goods should be distributed, and the delivery note passed to the Financial Accountant.*

2. Sorting out outgoing post

Objective: To make sure that outgoing mail is dealt with in a secure and controlled way.

a. *All outgoing mail should be put in envelopes and any enclosures checked to ensure that they are included.*

b. *Relevant information, such as PRIVATE AND CONFIDENTIAL, should be written clearly on the envelope.*

c. *The correct postage should be applied. Make sure that you have an up to date postage rate list.*

d. *All parcels should clearly show the receiver on the front and the sender (our company) on the back.*

e. *If you need to send a parcel by courier ensure that the contents are securely wrapped.*

f. *Make sure that you know the value of the contents of the parcel and its approximate weight.*

g. *Contact the courier company and ask them to collect the parcel. Ask them for the cost of the service.*

h. *You will need to give the value and weight so that they can calculate the cost of the delivery.*

i. *Complete a purchase order form with the courier, parcel details and cost, and give this to the Financial Accountant.*

3. Answering the telephone

Objective: To ensure that all telephone answering is done in a consistent way, to always delight the customer

a. *Ensure that someone is available to answer the telephone at all times.*

b. *Keep a telephone message pad beside every telephone for taking messages.*

c. *Always keep an up to date list of people who are out of the office, in meetings or not taking calls.*

d. *When answering the telephone smile before you answer and use the script agreed by the team members.*

e. *Don't interrogate the caller, and if the person that they would like to speak to is unavailable, then see if you can help.*

f. *If a call needs returning, remind the person returning the call to make sure that it is returned.*

4. Collecting outstanding debts

Here is how to collect outstanding debts from debtors – part of credit control

a. *Send customer a current account statement or gentle reminder*

b. *5 working days after sending the statement check to see whether the amount has been paid.*

c. *If the amount has not been paid, telephone the client and discuss the reason for non-payment, remind them of their credit terms, and agree a payment date.*

d. *Write a letter to the client summarising the telephone conversation and noting the agreed payment date.*

e. Make a note on the system of the date payment should be received.

f. If payment is not received by the agreed date telephone the client and remind them of your previous discussion.

g. Agree a date for payment (or direct debit/credit card if applicable).

h. Write a letter to the client summarising the telephone conversation and noting the agreed payment date.

i. Make a note on the system of the date payment should be received.

j. If payment is not received by the agreed date telephone the client.

k. Write a letter to the client summarising the telephone conversation and noting the date court proceedings will commence.

l. Make a note on the system of the date payment should be received.

m. If payment is not received within the specified time then continue with the County Court procedure.

n. Make arrangements to attend court.

KEY SKILLS, COMPETENCIES & ATTITUDES TO HELP YOU SUCCEED IN ACCOUNTING

Top accounting skills & competencies

Skilled people in any profession are very valuable. So let me take this opportunity to talk to you about some of the skills you should look to develop at this early formative years of your accounting career.

Attention to detail

Attention to detail is an essential requirement for a successful accounting career. The ability to notice one error, inconsistency or discrepancy can often lead to discovering other inaccuracies. On the other hand, missing a small detail can affect the integrity of the organisations financial records and may have dire consequences. It is therefore quite essential that you should have a detail-oriented approach to your work to ensure that financial records conform to standards, laws and regulations.

Analytical Skills

As an accountant, you must be analytical when examining documents and financial processes. The use of critical thinking skills to determine ways to make the organisation more financially efficient will be required of any good accountant.

My experience in working with many businesses is that; the analytical skills help you develop ways to reduce costs, increase revenues, improve profits and eliminate waste.

You will also have to carefully evaluate financial performance and investigate financial investments at some point in your accountancy career as you keep growing and that my friend, will call for excellent analytical skills.

Hopefully during your trainee years, you will be able to demonstrate this skill in greater measure

Good with numbers

From computing taxes and accurately preparing tax returns to completing balance sheet statements & reconciliations, accountants should be good with numbers. That is to say - be mathematically proficient. As an accountant you will be responsible for keeping track of your organisation's/company's spending and buying records, in addition to calculating budget amounts. These figures must be an accurate depiction of the organisation's finances.

Communication Skills

How are your written and verbal communication skills like?

You see, the accountant of the 21st century now interacts with a variety of people ranging from managers and directors to members of the accounting staff and various stakeholders in a business. It is therefore important that accountants must be able to clearly converse or correspond to ask questions and discuss issues or discrepancies quite easily. In addition, accountants offer advice and make recommendations regarding the best financial business decisions and being articulate and well presented will help a great deal here.

Accounting software skills

Gone are the days when accounting used to be done manually. Almost invariably, every business now uses some form of software to do their bookkeeping and accounts. From Excel to the more sophisticated ERP accounting software, accounting and financial analysis is now so much software based and the better you are in using any of these accounting software, the better you will be in your accounting career.

Accounting software all use the same basic principle of double entry, so if you are proficient in one, you will find it easy to learn any other accounting software relatively quickly.

I suggest therefore that you learn at least how to use one accounting software very well because that will act as a stepping stone for you learning other softwares should you change jobs and find that your new employer uses a different accounting software. At least know how to use one software proficiently.

Accuracy & speed

You need to be conscious of the fact that accounting is a very dynamic profession and at times very highly pressured. If you are looking to be successful in your accounting career, you've got to develop a reputation for speed and dependability (producing accurate & trustworthy information).

Time is the currency of the 21st century. Business today is very, very dynamic. Employers are less and less patient with slow incompetent employees because they recognise that customers will change suppliers overnight if someone else can serve them faster than the people they are currently dealing with.

So, your job, as you start developing your accountancy career is to develop a reputation for speed. Move fast on opportunities, move quickly when you see something that needs to be done. You've heard it said that whenever you want to get something done, give it to a busy man or woman.

Employees who have a reputation of moving quickly, attract more and more opportunities and possibilities to them and that is the kind of thing you want in the early years of your accountancy career development.

If you can combine your ability to determine your highest priority tasks with the commitment to getting it done quickly and accurately, you will find yourself progressing through your trainee years with flying colours and moving to the front/top of your accounting career and business fast and more doors and opportunities will open for you that you can't even imagine today.

The accounting job success triangle

With my experience I have now, being a professional accountant as well as and employer, I have come to realise that a successful career in accountancy is a combination of three things: - Skills/knowledge,

Experience & attitude.

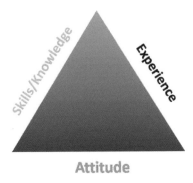

Fig. 15

Knowledge, experience and attitude; look at it as the three cornerstones that are necessary for you to build a formidable, exciting and enjoyable accountancy career.

Let me explain what I mean:

You see, succeeding in your accounting career is a combination of your theoretical knowledge/skill in accountancy coupled with your practical work experience but more importantly your attitude to life and work. I emphasise attitude here because in any endeavour of life, your attitude contributes about 80-90% of the success and enjoyment you will derive from it.

Come to think about it, you could be a genius as far as accounting is concerned and even have the most excellent and lofty practical experience there is to find, but if you have a terrible attitude, you will realise that not many people would like to work with you or have dealings with you in any way and that is not good news at all.

Attitudes that will help you succeed in accounting

So, let me talk to you a little bit about attitude since it is such a crucial aspect of your job success as an accountant just as it is in any area of your life. Your attitude goes a long way in determining what company of people you will keep, what actions you will take, how successful you will be in your accounting career and above all, how much and how deep you will enjoy life. Something worth exploring, wouldn't you agree? Yes, of course.

Look, I can guarantee you that your current attitude is either helping you move forward or is making you lag behind in life. The good news though is this; your attitude is 100% under your control and you can change it any time to help support your career progression.

Your Life only gets better when you get better, and since there is no limit on how much better you can become, there is no limit on how much better your life can become. True? Well, you be the judge.

Zig Ziglar once said; "*It's your attitude and not your aptitude that determines your altitude*".

Here then are some of the attitudes that I believe will help you make excellent progress in your accountancy career.

1. Attitude of gratitude

When you exude an attitude of gratitude at all times, you make people around you feel important. The truth is, everything you say or do that causes another person to feel better in any way also causes you to feel better to the same degree.

Haven't you realised that when you encourage, inspire, motivate someone else, you feel motivated, inspired and encouraged yourself? And guess what...

The converse is true, when you degrade, insult and abhor someone else, you feel the same too!

The need for appreciation is a deep subconscious desire of every individual you meet. When you satisfy this need, you will by all accounts become one of the most popular person in that person's world, and what is the key to expressing gratitude and appreciation? Simple, just say 'thank you' on every occasion.

You say thanks in a whole host of different ways: by giving compliments, admiration, giving encouragement, by unconditionally accepting people for who they are, by smiling, giving a hug, a pat on the back....., all these actions communicate one message ;-well done 'buddy' I am really proud of you'. If you become a finance manager, you should do more of this with your juniors.

In fact, the best way to ensure your happiness is to assist others experience their own. *"Those who bring Sunshine to others cannot keep it from themselves"* James Banie

Be a professional, happy, gregarious and friendly accountant. It will do you good.

2. A forgiving attitude

Jim Loehr & Tony Schwartz in their book; In the power of Full engagement, said *"The richer and deeper the source of our emotional recovery, the more we refill our reserves and the more resilient we become"*

You see, people are 100% emotional. People decide emotionally then justify logically. Emotion comes first. So when we are hurt, our emotions immediately take over and for some, this leads to prolonged periods of sulking and being grumpy and they will justify it logically by saying that they are hurt. What they seem not to understand is that a lot of their emotional energy which could otherwise be expended in some other productive venture is being put to waste on destructive tendencies.

So the faster they recover from any hurt through total and sincere forgiveness, the better for them.

I know it is not easy to forgive but I also know that it is difficult to enjoy life in an accounting career if you are hurting from the inside.

So if there is anyone who has hurt you even as you read this paragraph right now, it could be your parent(s), your spouse, your close friend, your sibling, your pastor, teacher, work mate, it could be anyone and everyone really, whoever it is, find it in your heart to forgive and release them, it's a very noble and an eternal act and the rewards are worth it.

Forgiveness is a choice and we all have to make that choice time and again if our relationships and careers are to be worth our time, effort and rewards thereof.

Be a forgiving accountant. Don't be a grumpy & bitter accountant.

3. Courageous attitude

Courage is a very admirable quality. Your boldness will help you get as much as you need in life. The bold move makes you seem larger and more powerful than you are. More than that, the bold draw attention and what draws attention, draws power. We simply cannot keep our eyes off the audacious can we? We can't wait to see their next bold move.

Every one admires the bold; no one honours the timid, isn't that true? Better still...

A courageous person is an upward and forward looking person, he/she faces the future without fear but with determination, not with doubt but with faith. He/she is willing to take great chances and reach for new horizons and remake the world around them. They recognise that there is more to their life than the ordinary, they take the status quo and turn it around. It is simply magnetic and very inspiring to be around them. The good news is that you can be one of those very courageous ones as well.

The courageous individuals teach us to have our horizons limitless and ultimately if we are to be true to our past, we also have to seize the future each and every day and courage will help us make the most of our time, abilities (effort), make the most of our opportunities that will ultimately help us make the most of our lives and accounting career.

And...

No matter how bitter the raw, how stony the accountancy road, courage enables us to persevere, not to falter or grow weary but to demand, strive and shape a better accountancy career for yourself! Simply refuse to give up on the idea of forward and upward move but ultimate triumph, despite the most extreme odds that you will sometimes face during your accountancy career. In some circumstances you will need a lot of courage to do the right thing that the code of ethics demand of you.

4. A compassionate attitude

Compassion makes you believable, it magnetises and magnifies the power of your faith and undeniably makes you very welcoming and attractive in the sight and hearts of many. Compassion moves the heavens on your behalf and bestows upon you the invisible power of influence and force of accomplishment.

Compassion naturally leads you to be a giver, it enhances the quality of benevolence - one of the hallmark characteristics of the truly superior person.

When you give freely and generously of yourself to others or for a cause, you feel more valuable and happier inside.

Here is a principle to remember when it comes to benevolence and compassion: "The more you give of yourself to others without expectation of return, the more good things there are that will come back to you from most unexpected sources"

You also realise that over time you are becoming more patient and understanding, less judgmental or demanding of others, you feel peaceful, confident and pleasant to be around. In a nutshell, you become a better and finer person and more importantly a compassionate accountant.

5. Integrity

Your Character is the most important thing that you develop in your entire life and your character is based on your integrity.

You develop integrity, and become a completely honest person, by practicing telling the truth to yourself and others in every situation.

It is imperative that your relationships and accountancy career are based on the foundation of truth and this can be done by developing the habit of living in truth with yourself and with everyone around you. Of course this does not mean that you will always be right 100% of the time, it however emphasises the fact that you endeavour to tell the truth, as you see or know it.

Others will learn to know that they can confidently rely on you and your word (and that is very important for an accountant). Though they may not like what you say on certain occasions, they will still know that you always speak the truth. This goes a very long way to earn you a great reputation in your accounting career and form a very solid foundation for your integrity.

Listen to what Shakespeare once wrote, *"To thine own self be true, and then it must follow, as the night the day, thou canst not then be false to any man"*.

In this day and age with the advancement of technology, CCTV and satellite, you cannot afford to be careless about how you conduct yourself or how you treat others or do business. To be successful nowadays is largely determined by the number of people who trust you and who are willing to work with you or give you credit if you are a borrower or help you during difficult times etc. Trust is very essential, and trust is earned not given, and you earn trust by being a person of integrity.

You must guard your integrity as a sacred thing, as the most important statement about you as an accountant.

As Brian Tracy once said; *"Whenever you are in doubt about a course of action, simply ask yourself, Is this the right thing to do?"* And then behave accordingly.

"Weakness of attitude becomes weakness of Character" – **A. Einstein**

6. A loving attitude

As Apostle Paul said in 1Corinthians 13:2-3 *"And though I have the gift of prophesy, and understand all mysteries, and all knowledge; and though I have all faith, so that I could remove mountains,......And though I bestow all my goods to feed the poor, and though I give my body to be burned, and have not Love, I am nothing"*

This is quite a profound statement, don't you think so? I believe it is one of the greatest and most challenging statement and message of all time.

What is interesting is that, you could actually possess all of the 5 preceding attitudes listed above, but without Love, your relationships and success in life are doomed to fail.

Jesus Christ emphasised this point of love so much, that He gave a new commandment: *"....Thou shalt love the lord thy god with all thy heart, and with all thy soul and with all thy mind.........., Thou shalt love thy neighbour as thyself"* Matthew 22:37-3

To love is a decision you make and should form a core part of your attitude in life and especially in your accounting career.

I think it is important to bear in mind what Jesus Christ said in the scripture above and also to embrace the golden Rule: *"Do unto others what you would have them do unto you".*

In closing on this aspect of attitudes of success in accountancy, I would like to say that; the way to a supper attitude and hence a great accountancy career at any time of the day and at any day of the week is to trust in God with all your heart and lean not on your own understanding.

I am not being spiritual here, but simply stating the obvious and plain truth. If you don't believe me, try it your way or any other way and see how far you can go being successful and happy at the same time.

I hope you will forever resolve to be a grateful, forgiving, courageous, compassionate, trustworthy and loving accountant. I really do hope so.

HELP & SUPPORT IN YOUR ACCOUNTING CAREER

Online accountancy resources available to help you succeed

Starting Point

- *AccountingWEB - The No1 web resource for the UK accountancy profession features the latest independent news, advice and guidance for the accounting profession.* www.accountingweb.co.uk

- *Accountancy Age- Finance, business and accountancy news, features, and resources for business and finance professionals.* www.accountancyage.com

- *Accountancy Magazine - The website of the leading monthly magazine for accountants.* www.accountancymagazine.com

The Associations

- *Institute of Chartered Accountants - The ICAEW is one of Europe›s major professional accountancy organisations.* www.icaew.co.uk

- *Association of Chartered Certified Accountants (ACCA) - The ACCA is the world›s largest and fastest-growing global professional accountancy body.* www.accaglobal.com

- *Association of International Accountants - An international accountancy and accountancy examining body, recognised in the UK under the Companies Act 1989.* www.aia.org.uk

- *Association of Accounting Technicians - The Association of Accounting Technician›s web site with information about the Association, benefits of membership, and student information.* www.aat.org.uk

Practical work experience

- *TD&A Certified Accountants – An accounting firm that also provides practical work experience training in accountancy.* www.tdanda.co.uk/careers

Visit their website at:

http://tdanda.co.uk/careers/

Looking for a Job?

- *Accountancy Age Jobs - UK finance jobs and accounting jobs at all levels, including public sector, practice and industry and commerce accountancy vacancies, auditing jobs and more.* www.accountancyagejobs.com

- *Accountant Careers - Specialist jobs board servicing Accounting and Finance Professionals across the UK and Ireland.* www.accountantcareers.co.uk

- *Gaap Web - UK based Accounting and Finance jobs site, containing current vacancies in Accountancy and Financial Services in the UK and beyond.* www.gaapweb.com

- *AccJobs - UK based Accounting, Banking and Finance job board, containing jobs for Accountants, Banking, and Financial professionals.* www.accjobs.com

- *Accountancy Job Board - UK based leading accountancy, finance and banking jobs boards. Search now and view the latest accounting vacancies or register for Jobs by Email and let the jobs come to you! www.accountancyjobsboard.co.uk*

- *Total jobs - UK based Accounting and Finance jobs site, containing current vacancies in Accountancy and Financial Services in the UK and beyond. www.totaljobs.com*

- *Libs recruitment - UK based leading accounts assistant & financial controller job board. Search now and view the latest accounting vacancies or register for Jobs by Email and let the jobs come to you! www.libsrecruitment.com*

Official Websites

- *HMRC – www.hmrc.gov.uk*
- *Direct.gov.uk*

AFTERWORD & CONCLUSION

It was a real honour speaking to you through the pages of this book. Thanks for listening to me.

If you found this book helpful, why not leave me your comment or feedback at sterling@sterlinglibs.com. I would really appreciate that.

I wish you a very fruitful and wonderful career as an accountant and if our path happen to cross somewhere on this planet, come over and say hi.

Sterling.

QUICK ORDER FORM

Postal Orders

Sterling Libs Books,
Level 33, 25 Canada Square,
Canary Wharf London, E14 5LQ

Telephone Orders
020 7038 8370 / 079 7055 0865

Email Orders
handbooks@sterlinglibs.com

Please send me the following books, disks or reports.

TICK	BOOK TITLE	PRICE (£)
☐	Work Experience in Accountancy - Workbook	£45.95
☐	The Accounts Assistant Job Manual – How to do the regular day to day tasks of an accounts assistant in Sage 50.	£65.95
☐	Month-End Accounting procedures	£40.95
☐	The Trainee Accountant – How to have a successful accounting career	£24.95
☐	Get your VAT return done in 5 steps	£25.95
☐	Business Intelligence – Start, Build & Run your own business and become financially independent.	£20.95
☐	Management Accounting practical guide	£45.95
☐	The Way to Get an Accounting Job in the UK - The 5 strategic steps	£22.95

PLEASE SEND MORE INFORMATION ON:

☐ Speaking/Seminars & accounting job fairs   ☐ Consulting & mentoring

YOUR DETAILS – FOR US TO SEND YOU THE BOOK(S) YOU'VE ORDERED

Name:

Address:

City/Town: **Postcode:**

Contact No.:   **Email:**

POSTAGE & PACKAGING OF £5 APPLY IF WITHIN UK AND £9 FOR INTERNATIONAL ORDERS

QUICK ORDER FORM

Postal Orders

Sterling Libs Books,
Level 33, 25 Canada Square,
Canary Wharf London, E14 5LQ

Telephone Orders
020 7038 8370 / 079 7055 0865

Email Orders
handbooks@sterlinglibs.com

Please send me the following books, disks or reports.

TICK	BOOK TITLE	PRICE (£)
☐	Work Experience in Accountancy - Workbook	£45.95
☐	The Accounts Assistant Job Manual – How to do the regular day to day tasks of an accounts assistant in Sage 50.	£65.95
☐	Month-End Accounting procedures	£40.95
☐	The Trainee Accountant – How to have a successful accounting career	£24.95
☐	Get your VAT return done in 5 steps	£25.95
☐	Business Intelligence – Start, Build & Run your own business and become financially independent.	£20.95
☐	Management Accounting practical guide	£45.95
☐	The Way to Get an Accounting Job in the UK - The 5 strategic steps	£22.95

PLEASE SEND MORE INFORMATION ON:

☐ Speaking/Seminars & accounting job fairs   ☐ Consulting & mentoring

YOUR DETAILS – FOR US TO SEND YOU THE BOOK(S) YOU'VE ORDERED

Name:

Address:

City/Town: **Postcode:**

Contact No.:   **Email:**

POSTAGE & PACKAGING OF £5 APPLY IF WITHIN UK AND £9 FOR INTERNATIONAL ORDERS

18584805R00050

Printed in Great Britain
by Amazon